THE RAINBOW FLAMINGO

Mam,
This one was always for you –
you always made me proud of
my feathers. It breaks my heart
you aren't here to see it
published. Sleep tight,
love you. C.E. x

To Melissa,
thank you for
the rainbows.
C.P. x

SIMON & SCHUSTER
Celebrating 100 Years of Publishing Since 1924
First published in Great Britain in 2024 by Simon & Schuster UK Ltd
1st Floor, 222 Gray's Inn Road, London WC1X 8HB

A CIP catalogue record for this book is available from the British Library upon request

ISBN: 978-1-4711-8173-3 (HB)
ISBN: 978-1-4711-8172-6 (PB)
ISBN: 978-1-4711-8174-0 (eBook)

Printed in China
1 3 5 7 9 10 8 6 4 2

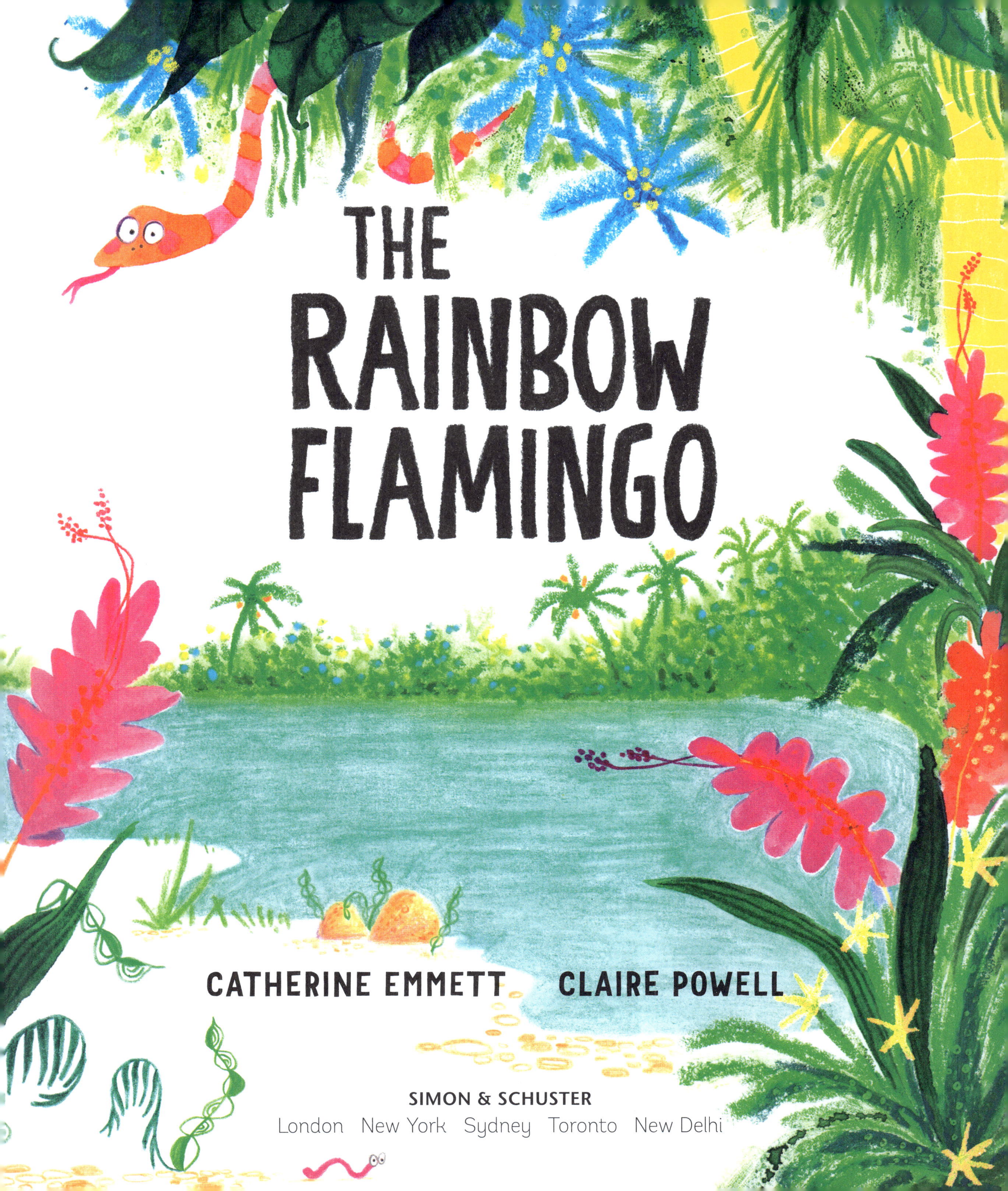

THE RAINBOW FLAMINGO

CATHERINE EMMETT   CLAIRE POWELL

SIMON & SCHUSTER
London New York Sydney Toronto New Delhi

Right on the shore of the Great Zumbo Lake,
One thousand flamingos were starting to wake.

Some ruffled their feathers and some took a drink,
But ALL of the thousand flamingos were pink.

The pink colour came from the shrimp that they ate,
They gobbled it up at a frightening rate!
That's just how it was, how it always had been –
A non-pink flamingo had never been seen!

But one young flamingo, Adele was her name,
Knew under HER wings something wasn't the same.

Whilst quite unremarkably pink
from outside . . .

Inside were some **colours** she struggled to hide!

She'd tried eating up all the shrimp that she could,
But somehow it just didn't do what it should . . .

She fretted and feared what the others would think,
If anyone saw underneath wasn't **pink**!

The yearly Flamboyance was coming up quick,
Which made poor Adele feel all worried and sick.
Flamingos competed from all over town,
But only the pinkest would take home the crown!

This year Adele's class would be dancing a dance,
They'd all pirouette and they'd twirl and they'd prance.
Adele knew for sure there'd be nowhere to hide –
She'd never keep all of her colours inside!

Her friends were excited, they chattered away,
And practised the steps for their dance the next day.
She watched them all laughing, but felt so alone,

She made her excuses and . . .

. . . headed back home.

Adele felt all anxious, so sought out her mum,
She summoned her courage – but then she said,

"Ummmmm . . ."

Her mum had been sticking some shrimp onto sticks,
And now she was giving some cake dough a mix,

"Yes, darling what is it? I've lots to prepare,
And haven't a clue which **tiara** to wear!"

Adele felt her feelings well up in her heart,
But just couldn't seem to find where she should start.
She felt all choked up and the words wouldn't come,

"It isn't important, so don't worry, Mum . . ."

Adele slunk away to a quieter spot,
Her eyes felt all teary, her cheeks felt all hot.
Perhaps she could find some new food or a drink,
That maybe, just might, make those feathers turn pink . . .

And so, she set off to find new things to eat,
Some tasted quite sour,

whilst some tasted sweet.

Some foods were all spiky and
quite hard to munch,

Whilst some were determined
they wouldn't be lunch!

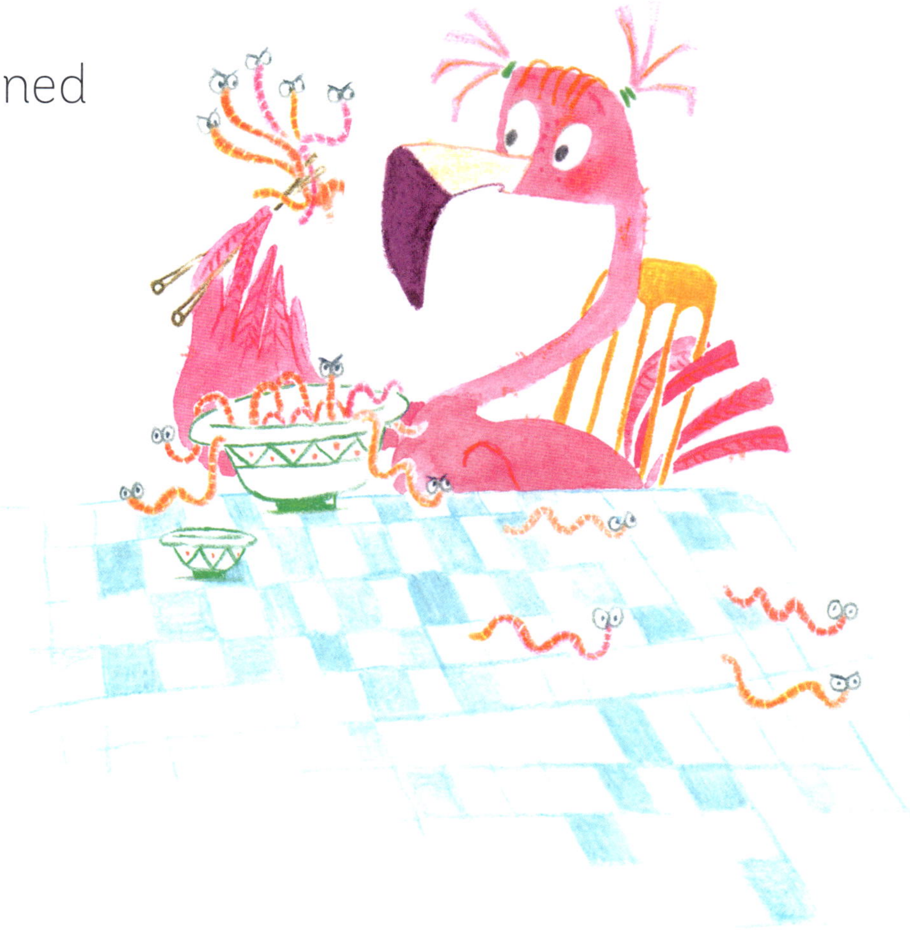

Some made her eyes water
with each single bite,

But one made her tummy feel really not right . . .

Her stomach felt **swirly**,

then **whirly**,

then **sick**.

She had to get home and she'd better go quick!

By this point, Adele was decidedly green,
The least pink flamingo that ever there'd been!

She wobbled and worried, "Oh what have I done!"
But just as she panicked – she spotted her mum!

She tried to explain, but she barely could speak,
As long-held-back tears slowly rolled down her beak.

"Oh darling, what is it?
Let's get you back home."

At last Adele saw that she wasn't alone,

And this time she COULD find the right way to start –
Adele didn't stop 'til she'd poured out her heart.
Her mum sat and listened, "Adele we love YOU,
We couldn't care less if you're green, pink or blue!"

Adele dried her tears feeling better at last,
A lifetime of hiding was now in her past!

The yearly Flamboyance began the next day,
And soon all the dancing was well underway!
The party was swinging,

the music was loud!

Adele gave a gulp when she saw the huge crowd.

Her mum squeezed her close as they made their way in,
"Your dance will be starting, you'd better begin!"

Adele felt all sweaty, but took up her place,
And focused upon her mum's proud, beaming face.

She took a deep breath and she thrust her wings high!

She danced and she pranced and she leapt for the sky!
When all of the crowd saw the rainbowy sight,

They **honked** and they **flapped**

and they **clapped with delight!**

That year the Flamboyance danced right through the town,
The Rainbow Flamingo had taken the crown!

CHEMIST
Fleurs
BREAD
GREENS
VEG
FRUIT
Antiques

And later Adele found she wasn't alone,
As some of her friends had some hues of their own!

So, don't be afraid,
wear your feathers with pride,

We **ALL** have some
fabulous colours inside!